THE RECIPES FROM CIMARRON FALLS

The Recipes From Cimarron Falls
© 2023 by Julie Adkison

All rights reserved. No portion of this book may be reproduced, stored in a retrieval system, or transmitted in any form or by any means—electronic, mechanical, photocopy, recording, scanning, or other—except for brief quotations in critical reviews or articles, without the prior written permission of the publisher.

ISBN: 979-8-9885695-2-7

Cover and interior design by Kenny Holcomb
Author photography by Designed Identities/Audrey Noe

Printed in the United States of America

JULIE ADKISON

THE RECIPES FROM CIMARRON FALLS

NASHVEGAS NATIVE PUBLISHING

～ TABLE OF CONTENTS ～

INTRODUCTION   1

1. SOUP & APPETIZERS

The Sage Squash Soup	5
The Nutty Nightcap	7
Bountiful Charcuterie	9
Open Face Tomato Sandwiches	11
Cucumber Sandwiches	12
Chicken Bacon Bites	13
Julie's Famous Guacamole	14

2. BREAKFAST

Bea's Breakfast Casserole	17
Blueberry Pancakes	19
Garlic Cheese Grits	21
Betsy's Cinnamon Rolls	23

3. MAIN COURSE

The Frisian Forest Floor (Winter Grain Bowl)	27
Ryan's Traditional Chicken Enchiladas	29
Pad Thai That Binds	31
Marinated Grilled Flank Steak	35

4. ALL ABOUT SIDES

Sweet Potato Casserole w/Pecans	39
T's Skillet Cornbread	41
Cornbread Dressing	43
Betsy's Pineapple Casserole	45
Green Bean Bundles	47
Potato Cheese Casserole	49

5. DESSERT

Pecan Pie	53
Pumpkin Cheesecake	55
Glazed Teacake	57
Four Layer Dessert	59
Julie's Chocolate Chip Cookies	61

ABOUT THE AUTHOR — 64

INTRODUCTION

I have always loved cooking — almost as much as I love writing. I have early childhood memories of my mom, "T," patiently letting me help her prepare meals. I didn't set out to write a "culinary mystery," which is one of the classifications Cimarron Falls has been given. I just knew that my character, Christina, was a chef and I knew that the Davidsons would have bonding moments, as well as tense moments, over meals together. That resulted in a lot of references to food.

When people started asking where they could find the recipes from the book, I knew that some kind of cookbook was inevitable. This is not an extensive cookbook by any means, but you are now in possession of recipes that you will use over and over.

It is an honor to be sharing so many of my family's most loved recipes. We are all partial to our mom's cooking. Almost all of the recipes are really hers. It's no surprise that she has gained quite the reputation as a cook from many friends along the way.

I hope you enjoy these recipes as much as we do.

Julie

I. SOUP & APPETIZERS

The Sage Squash Soup

Tears started to sting her eyes, but Christina shook them away and quickly finished preparing a hearty pot of butternut squash and sage soup, which she had playfully named The Sage Squash. Naming her menu items was a secondary creative outlet next to creating the dishes. The Sage Squash was a play on words, alluding to a bowl of wisdom.

Serves 6

1 large butternut squash, peeled and diced (or 2 containers pre-cut from produce section – I have also used 2 packages of the frozen spirals)
2 onions, quartered
32 oz. chicken broth
14.5 ounce can of coconut milk
1 tablespoon sage, minced (or ½ teaspoon ground sage)
2 teaspoons garlic powder
1 teaspoon curry powder
½ teaspoon lemon pepper
¼ teaspoon cinnamon

In a large pot, bring all ingredients except coconut milk into a boil. Reduce to low heat and simmer for 20 minutes.

Add the coconut milk.

Puree with immersible blender or transfer in batches to blender or food processer.

Add more chicken broth or a little water if you want a thinner consistency.

The Nutty Nutcap

Another popular soup was a cauliflower, bacon, and hazelnut blend she titled The Nutty Nightcap. This blend seemed to lull one into a calm state with its precise amount of nutmeg, bacon, and hazelnuts blended into a liquid sleep aid. People swore it made them feel as if they'd taken a sedative, and it became a popular dinner item.

Serves 6

1 head of cauliflower, roughly chopped (or 3 bags frozen cauliflower)
1 large onion, diced
1 clove garlic, minced
2 tablespoons butter
½ teaspoon salt
¼ teaspoon pepper
1/8 teaspoon nutmeg
½ teaspoon lemon pepper
2 strips of bacon
32 oz. chicken broth
½ cup half & half
¼ cup chopped, roasted hazelnuts (my local Kroger carries them, but if you can't find them you could substitute with pecans, walnuts, almonds or pistachios.)

Fry bacon in large soup pot.

Remove bacon, then chop and set aside.

Leave the bacon grease in the pot.

Add onions and garlic to pot and saute in the bacon grease for 3 minutes or until they are starting to become tender.

Add cauliflower and all other ingredients *except for the half & half.*

Bring to boil, then turn burner to low and simmer for 20 minutes.

Add the half & half then puree with immersible hand blender or use blender or food processor.

Top soup with 2 teaspoons each of chopped bacon and roasted hazelnuts.

Bountiful Charcuterie

"Stop, please. Not now, Erica. I can't go there. The Bakers are going to be at our door in minutes." She opened the refrigerator, picked up a bowl of grapes, and placed it on the counter, then set about arranging a charcuterie board.

Serves 6 to 10+

Gruyere Cheese, sliced
Mini Marinated Fresh Mozzarella Balls
Blueberry Encrusted Goat Cheese
Sharp Cheddar Cheese, sliced
Sliced Salami
Sliced Pepperoni
Sliced Prosciutto
Rosemary Marcona Almonds
Honey
Whole Grain Mustard
Fruit spread such as Fig Jam
One bunch of grapes
Assorted crackers (I use rice crackers, water crackers, wheat crackers, and then something rustic with nuts and berries in it)

On a large decorative tray start arranging the cheese and meat where they are overlapping a little. I like for it to look bountiful by piling it up. I tend to group the cheese together and the meat together. I also like to put the grapes on the tray even if they are partially on top of something else. The green (or red) of the grapes is pretty with the colors of the cheese and meat.

I have a crazy assortment of small ramekins and bowls that I put the honey, mustard, mozzarella balls, etc. in. I have even used shot glasses or dessert bowls. If these don't fit on the main tray, they look good gathered around the edges of the tray along with small bowls of crackers. I have a good collection of cheese knives, little spoons, forks and spreaders. But you can improvise with regular everyday cutlery or even plasticware.

Note: Obviously you can use different kinds of cheese and meat (and everything else) than what is listed above. I'm just showing you how I do it to give you inspiration for your own.

Open Face Tomato Sandwiches

Makes 20 sandwiches

10 slices white bread
5 or 6 small tomatoes (such as Roma or Campari), sliced
1 cup mayonnaise
½ cup bacon pieces (I use the bagged kind)
2-inch round cookie cutter

Combine mayonnaise and bacon pieces.

Flatten bread slices with rolling pen and cut two circles from each slice of bread.

Spread 2 teaspoons of mayo/bacon mixture on each round.

Top each round with one slice of tomato.

Open Face Cucumber Sandwiches

Makes 20 sandwiches

10 slices white bread
1 English Cucumber
½ small onion, finely diced
8 oz. cream cheese, softened
½ t. salt
¼ t. pepper
2 dashes hot sauce
2-inch round cookie cutter

Cut the cucumber in half.

Peel and thinly slice one half – set aside.

Deseed and dice the other half.

Stir onion, diced cucumber, cream cheese, salt, pepper and hot sauce together until combined.

Flatten bread slices with rolling pen and cut out two circles from each piece.

Smear 2 teaspoons of cream cheese mixture on the rounds.

Top with cucumber slices.

Chicken Bacon Bites

Makes about 25 bites

Oven 375

3 large chicken breasts diced – about 8 or 9 pieces per breast
½ pound bacon cut in thirds
1 jar mild (or no heat) pickled jalapeno slices
Fajita seasoning (from packet or spice aisle)
9"x13" baking pan

Assemble bites by placing one jalapeno slice on a piece of chicken, then wrapping the small slice of bacon around it.

Place in baking pan and repeat until all ingredients are used.

Sprinkle fajita seasoning liberally on top.

Bake for 45 min or until chicken is cooked through and bacon is browning

Note: These little finger sandwiches and chicken bites do not make an appearance in the book, but they were quite the hit at my book release party that my sister, Betsy, threw for me. Our 75-plus guests ate hundreds of these appetizers along with charcuterie, brownies and petit fours.

Julie's Famous Guacamole

Erica and Ryan hurried through the upscale Mountain Market, picking up items they had forgotten at City Market in Montrose. Ryan had offered to make dinner. She'd decided on chicken enchiladas but was short one can of diced tomatoes, avocados for guac, and a bag of tortilla chips.

Serves 6 to 8

3 medium avocados
¼ cup diced red onion
Juice of ½ a lime
½ teaspoon salt
1 small tomato, diced

Dice and roughly mash avocado.

Mix in red onion, salt, and lime.

Gently stir in tomatoes.

Note: I am known for my guac. I have always liked it simple and sort of chunky. I've been making it for years, but I recently saw a cooking show where my favorite chef, Alex Guarnaschelli, makes it the exact same way!

2. BREAKFAST

Bea's Breakfast Casserole

The smell of a breakfast casserole wafting down the stairs pulled Christina out of her morning drowse. Through all of her years of being a chef, her tastes had grown more sophisticated, but she was certain she'd never outgrow her love of casseroles. This particular one was Bea's specialty: sausage, egg, and cheese baked to perfection on top of buttered white bread in a casserole dish. She could follow her mom's recipe to the letter, but it never tasted as good as when she prepared it. She and her sisters joked with Bea that there must be secret ingredients she had failed to share.

Serves 6 to 8

6 slices white bread, with crust removed
3 tablespoons butter
1 lb. mild sausage
6 eggs
12 oz. sharp cheddar cheese, grated
2 cups half & half
½ teaspoon salt
½ teaspoon pepper
1 teaspoon dry mustard

Butter bread and cut in fourths.

Line bottom of 9x13 casserole dish with the buttered bread.

Brown sausage and drain well.

Sprinkle sausage over bread.

Top with cheese.

Beat eggs and add remaining ingredients to them.

Pour mixture over cheese.

Cover with plastic wrap and chill 8 hours or overnight in fridge.

Bake 20-25 minutes at 350.

Start in cold oven.

Note: Of course, this is my mom's wonderful breakfast casserole. My sisters and I really do think she's holding out on us on certain ingredients. We are just not able to make it taste as good as hers. She swears this is the complete recipe.

Christina's Blueberry Pancakes

Christina cranked out blueberry pancakes like the pro that she was. Plates of bacon, eggs, and fruit were passed around along with small pottery pitchers of warm maple syrup. It was such a moment of happiness for Bea that it was almost as if nothing was wrong.

Makes 12 to 14 pancakes

1 ½ cups flour
1 teaspoon salt
3 tablespoons sugar
1 ¾ teaspoons baking powder

2 eggs
3 tablespoons butter, melted
1 cup milk
½ cup blueberries
Vegetable oil

Combine all ingredients in medium bowl being careful not to over stir.

Heat a couple tablespoons of vegetable oil in skillet or griddle until drops of water pass the sizzle test.

Using a ¼ cup measure, ladle onto skillet being careful not to let the pancakes run together. When pancakes are placed sprinkle blueberries over them. When bubbles rise to the top and break, flip them over. The second side will not take as long to cook as the first.

My family serves them with butter and heated maple syrup.

Note: Oh, how my dad loved blueberry pancakes. He was often on restrictive diets due to multiple health concerns, but it was no holds barred when it came to the pancakes. I even have childhood memories of my mom making them on the camping stove at the Colorado campsite.

Garlic Cheese Grits

In addition to the breakfast casserole, she had a plate piled with bacon, a big bowl of cheese grits, and a platter of cut-up oranges, strawberries, and pineapple.

Serves 6 to 8

Oven 325

1 cup grits
6 oz. American cheese, grated
1 teaspoon garlic powder
2 eggs
Half & half
½ stick of butter

Cook grits according to package directions in medium pan.

Add cheese, garlic powder and butter and mix well.

Beat eggs in a 1 cup liquid measuring cup. Fill cup the rest of the way with half & half.

Add to grits and mix well.

Pour into 2-quart greased casserole dish.

Bake for 25 minutes until set.

Betsy's Cinnamon Rolls

As unseasonal as it was, there was something cozy about the November rain today. It also happened to be unseasonably warm, so Erica, Bea, and Ryan gathered around the table on the covered deck, coffee in hand.

Scooting her chair farther away from the edge, where rain bounced off the railing, Bea asked, "Do you think we can hear the buzzer from out here? I just put some cinnamon rolls in the oven."

Makes 12 Cinnamon Rolls

Oven 450

1 cup flour
2 teaspoons baking powder
½ teaspoon salt
3 tablespoons shortening
1/3 cup milk
1/3 cup sugar
1 teaspoon cinnamon
¼ cup butter

In a small bowl combine sugar and cinnamon – set aside.

In a mixing bowl combine flour, baking powder and salt.

Cut shortening into flour mixture.

Add milk and mix well.

Roll out into a rectangle shape, very thin.

Dot butter on dough.

Sprinkle with cinnamon sugar mixture.

Roll up jelly roll style.

Slice off about 1" at a time and place each piece in greased muffin tin.

Bake for 10 minutes.

Note: These are not your typical yeasty, puffy cinnamon rolls. Instead, they have a biscuit consistency which is why they have always been my favorite. My sister, Betsy, got this recipe in Home Economics class in high school! They are still as good today as they were in the late eighties.

3. MAIN COURSE

The Frisian Forest Bowl
(AKA WINTER GRAIN BOWL)

Christina had been working on a review-worthy meal of roasted sweet potatoes, peppers, and onions to layer over a bed of brown rice and arugula, topped with a citrus-balsamic drizzle. The rice in this dish reminded her of soil; the arugula greens were the sprouting buds coming forth from the earth. The potatoes and other vegetables were like the animals running around the woods, searching for the fresh green sprigs to eat. She laughed at the vision the dish created in her mind's eye. It was tasty though. She should add this one to her winter menu in December. Maybe call it The Frisian Forest Floor. When her clientele asked the meaning—and they always did—she'd say, "All these things came from the ground, so have at it you vegans!" Translating the menu titles had become something of a game to Christina's guests. They tried to guess and were often rewarded with a free drink of choice if they nailed it.

Makes 6 servings

3 cups cooked brown rice
6 cups arugula
3 large sweet potatoes, peeled and diced
2 green bell peppers, diced
1 large onion, diced
½ cup pistachios

For Citrus-Balsamic Dressing:
¼ cup olive oil
¼ cup balsamic vinegar
¼ cup honey
Juice from half an orange
Juice from half a lemon

Roast sweet potatoes, peppers and onions on greased baking sheet at 425 degrees for 20 min., stirring after 10 min. Vegetables should be tender and even starting to crisp.

Put ½ cup brown rice in a medium bowl.

Next add 1 cup arugula.

Roasted veggies are next, followed by 1 tablespoon pistachios.

Repeat for all 6 bowls.

Mix together all dressing ingredients in a jar with a lid.

Shake well, then drizzle over bowls.

Ryan's Traditional Chicken Enchiladas

Erica and Bea sat at the kitchen bar eating chips, salsa, and Ryan's guacamole while Ryan assembled the enchiladas. Holding each corn tortilla carefully with tongs, she lightly browned both sides in the skillet. Each one was filled with chicken, green chiles, tomatoes, and cheese. Next, she lined the enchiladas neatly in the casserole dish and poured more sauce over them, then spread sour cream on top and sprinkled them with a generous layer of Monterey Jack. She did all of this while singing and dancing around the kitchen. Ryan radiated pure joy, and it made Erica's heart sing.

Makes 4 to 6 servings

Oven 325

4 large, boneless chicken breasts, cooked and diced
2 tablespoons butter
1 large onion, chopped
1 clove garlic, minced
1 (16 oz.) can diced tomatoes, undrained
1 (8 oz.) can tomato sauce
1 (4 oz.) can diced green chiles
1 teaspoon cumin
½ teaspoon oregano
½ teaspoon salt
3 cups (12 oz.) shredded Monterey Jack cheese, divided use
1 ½ cups sour cream, divided use
Vegetable oil for heating tortillas
12 (6"-8") corn tortillas

In a large skillet, melt butter and add onion and garlic.

Saute' for 3-5 minutes.

Stir in undrained tomatoes, tomato sauce, green chiles, cumin, oregano and salt.

Simmer on low heat for 30 minutes.

Stir in chicken, 2 cups of the cheese, and 1 cup of the sour cream.

Heat ½ inch oil in small skillet.

Dip each tortilla in the hot oil – about 10-15 seconds on each side.

Set aside on plate with paper towel on it until all 12 are done.

To assemble enchiladas put tortilla on small plate and scoop 1/3 cup of chicken mixture onto it.

Roll it up and place seam side down in greased 9x13 baking dish.

Line the enchiladas side by side so that they're touching.

Pour any remaining sauce over the enchiladas and bake for 20 minutes.

Spread the remaining sour cream and cheese on top and bake for 10 more minutes.

Pad Thai That Binds

"Oh, ha-ha, I call it Pad Thai That Binds. Noodles are a comfort food in every culture, and comfort food seems to bring people together, especially family," Christina explained, basking in the admiration of her mom and sisters.

Makes 6 to 8 servings

Oven 350

For the chicken:
3 large chicken breasts
1 tablespoon soy sauce
½ teaspoon sesame oil
½ garlic powder

Heat oven to 350

Place chicken breasts in small baking dish.

Pour soy sauce and sesame oil over chicken.

Sprinkle garlic powder on top.

Bake for 25 min. until cooked through

Dice and set aside.

For the noodles:
8 oz. package linguine rice noodles (I use Thai Kitchen)

Large pot of boiling water

2 eggs

½ cup grated carrots

1 cup sliced green onion

3 tablespoons vegetable oil, divided use.

Put noodles in boiling water and turn off burner.

Let set for 15 minutes.

Drain noodles in colander.

Heat 1 tablespoon oil over medium-high heat in wok or skillet.

Scramble the egg, remove from pan and dice – set aside.

Heat 2 tablespoons oil over medium-high heat.

Saute' green onions and carrots for 3-5 minutes.

Add noodles to pan and toss to combine with eggs, onions and carrots.

For the sauce:
1 teaspoon sesame oil
2 teaspoon rice vinegar
Small jar pad Thai sauce *(I use Thai Kitchen or Kroger brand)*
½ cup chicken broth
2 tablespoons brown sugar
1 cup sweet chili sauce *(I use P.F. Chang's)*

In a medium bowl whisk together all ingredients then pour into pan over noodles.

Simmer for 10 minutes, stirring occasionally.

For topping:
1/4 cup cilantro, chopped
½ cup peanuts, crushed

After plating noodles, sprinkle 1 tablespoon crushed peanuts on top, followed by 2 teaspoons cilantro.

Marinated Grilled Flank Steak

"Hmm. I'll have to think about the perfect dish to serve the parents of the dead girl Dad eavesdropped on," Christina said a little too sarcastically.

Makes 6 to 8 servings

3 lbs. flank steak *(I usually get two 1.5 lb. steaks)*
1 clove garlic
1 teaspoon salt
1 tablespoon olive oil
1 tablespoon tomato paste or ketchup
3 tablespoons soy sauce
½ teaspoon oregano
½ teaspoon pepper
Plastic wrap

In a shallow, medium bowl use a fork to mash garlic into salt until it becomes a pulp.

Add the rest of the ingredients and stir until combined.

Spread out 2 large pieces of plastic wrap on counter for each steak.

Score steaks deeply in a criss-cross pattern on both sides.

Spread marinade over both sides of steaks.

Wrap the plastic wrap snugly around the steaks and put in gallon sealable bag.

Marinate overnight or for at least 6 hours.

Grill steaks over direct heat for 2 minutes, then rotate 5 degrees for two more minutes (this will create grill marks).

Flip steaks over and repeat above process.

Transfer to indirect heat and set timer for 5 minutes. At this time steaks should be medium.

Leave on grill longer if you like it more well-done.

Let steaks rest for 5 minutes then cut against the grain in thin strips.

Note: I envision that this is what the Davidsons served the Bakers when they came over for dinner. It is my family's go-to Birthday dinner, special occasion dinner and company's coming over dinner. I recommend serving it with Potato Cheese Casserole and Green Bean Bundles which can be found in the All About Sides chapter.

4. ALL ABOUT SIDES

FROM THANKSGIVING, TO FANCY DINNERS AND BEYOND

These are the side dish recipes that I think the Davidsons served for Thanksgiving and the dinner party with the Bakers. While my family has very strong opinions on what sides should be served, we have never been very attached to a certain turkey recipe, so I didn't include one. Turkey recipes can easily be found in other cookbooks and on the internet. However, these sides I'm sharing with you are family gold!

Sweet Potato Casserole with Pecans

*Everyone laughed in agreement, then Christina interrupted,
"I hate to crack the whip, but we have a lot of food to make today.
Who wants to be on sweet potato–peeling duty?"
Groans arose in protest over the dirty, tedious task.*

Serves 6 to 8

Oven 350

3 lbs. sweet potatoes, peeled and sliced
1/3 cup brown sugar
2 tablespoons butter
2 tablespoons frozen orange juice concentrate
1 ½ teaspoons cinnamon
½ teaspoon salt
2 large eggs, beaten
¼ cup chopped pecans

Put sliced sweet potatoes in large pot and cover with water.

Bring to boil then simmer on low for 20 minutes.

Pour out water and add all ingredients *except for eggs and pecans.*

Beat with hand mixer until all ingredients are combined and sweet potatoes are smooth.

Add eggs and beat until combined.

Spread sweet potato mixture in greased 11x7 casserole dish.

Sprinkle pecans on top.

Bake for 45 minutes.

T's Skillet Cornbread

Serves 8

Oven 450 (Spray iron skillet with cooking spray and let heat up in oven while oven is preheating. You want the skillet really hot.)

2 cups cornmeal (white or yellow are equally good)
2 teaspoons baking powder
½ teaspoon baking soda
1 teaspoon salt
3 tablespoons sugar
4 tablespoons vegetable oil
1 ½ cups buttermilk
2 eggs, beaten
3 tablespoons water

Preheat oven to 450 and place greased iron skillet in oven immediately to heat up.

While skillet is heating up in oven, combine all ingredients in medium mixing bowl.

Pour batter into hot iron skillet.

Bake for 15-20 minutes until golden brown.

We cut it into 8 pieces and butter each piece as soon as it comes out of the oven. You don't need to do this if using the cornbread for Cornbread Dressing.

Cornbread Dressing

"Hey, Erica? You wanna come in here and help me make the dressing?" Christina hollered from the kitchen. Erica was nowhere near the cook that Christina was, but she had the patience to chop the ten onions and entire bunch of celery that Bea's dressing recipe called for.

Serves 8 to 10

Oven 350

1 large pan of T's Skillet Cornbread
5 onions, chopped
½ bunch of celery, sliced
6 tablespoons butter
2 cups chicken broth
1 small can Evaporated milk
3 eggs, beaten until frothy
½ stack saltine crackers, crushed
1 teaspoon salt
½ teaspoon pepper
1 ½ teaspoons poultry seasoning
(Water as needed to thin out)

Crumble cornbread in big chunks into large
  mixing bowl.
Pour broth over cornbread and let it sit for 5 minutes to
  soak up liquid.
While cornbread is soaking, saute' onions and celery
  in butter in a medium skillet.

Add onions, celery and all other ingredients to cornbread mixture and mix well. Add a ¼ cup water if it seems like consistency is too thick. It should pour easily into 9x13 baking dish.

Bake for 30-40 minutes or until set and starting to brown.

Note: I halved the recipe for this cookbook. Unless you are feeding an army, you will not need the amount that the Davidsons were making for their Thanksgiving dinner.

Betsy's Pineapple Casserole

Serves 6 to 8

Oven 350

1 (20 oz.) can pineapple chunks
3 tablespoons reserved pineapple juice from can
3 tablespoons flour
½ cup sugar
1 cup cheddar cheese, grated
1 cup crushed Ritz crackers
½ stick butter, melted

Drain pineapple chunks, reserving 3 tablespoons of the juice.

In a small bowl mix crushed Ritz and melted butter – set aside.

Mix juice, flour, sugar and cheese in medium mixing bowl.

Add pineapple chunks.

Pour into 11x7 casserole dish.

Spread Ritz/butter mixture on top.

Bake for 20 minutes or until crackers are golden brown.

Note: I admit that I was a holdout on this casserole until recent years. When I finally tried it, I couldn't believe I had been missing out on it all those years. Betsy is an excellent cook and she knows what is good. I should have trusted her sooner.

Green Bean Bundles

Serves 6 to 8

Oven 350

3 cans whole green beans
¾ pound bacon
1 stick butter
½ cup brown sugar
½ teaspoon salt
¼ teaspoon pepper
½ teaspoon garlic powder

In a small saucepan, combine butter, brown sugar, salt, pepper and garlic powder.

Cook over medium heat until butter is melted, stirring occasionally.

When combined, turn burner on low.

While sauce is cooking, assemble bundles.

Take 1/3 bacon slice and wrap around 5 or 6 green beans.

Place bundles in greased 9x13 casserole dish.

Repeat until you've used all the green beans.

Pour sauce over bundles.

Bake for 45 minutes.

Note: These are great for Thanksgiving and the holidays OR a fancy dinner when company is coming over. Guests cannot resist the sweet and savory taste combination!

Potato Cheese Casserole

Serves 8

Oven 325

6 medium Russet potatoes
1 stick butter, melted
8 oz. sharp cheddar cheese, grated
2 cups sour cream
1 teaspoon salt
½ teaspoon pepper
1/3 cup chopped green onions or chives

Scrub potatoes well and boil with skins on in large pot.

Potatoes should be tender, but still slightly firm. When skins start "cracking" you know they are done.

Let potatoes cool for best results.

Remove skins by peeling them off with fingers.

Grate potatoes into large mixing bowl.

Add all ingredients and mix thoroughly, but gently.

Scoop into 11x7 casserole dish.

Bake 30 minutes or until starting to brown.

Note: this delicious casserole is sort of a pain to make, but the payoff is well worth it. People LOVE it! It is great with the Flank Steak and Green Bean Bundles.

5. JUST DESSERTS

Pecan Pie

"It's dessert time!" Christina announced. "Dad wants a little sliver of both cheesecake and the pecan pie. Who else is ready?"

Makes 2 pies, serves 16

Oven 350

¾ cup sugar
1 ½ cups white Karo syrup
3 eggs
3 tablespoons flour
3 tablespoons butter, melted
1 ½ cups chopped pecans
1 tablespoon vanilla
2 (9 inch) pre-made pie shells

Divide pecans into the two pie shells.

Beat eggs, sugar and Karo together.

Add the rest of the ingredients and mix well.

Pour over pecans into the pie shells.

Bake at 325 for 45 minutes or until set.

Pumpkin Cheesecake

"When should I make the pumpkin cheesecake?"
Sophia asked from her perch on the barstool.
"Maybe tonight?" Christina suggested. "After we clear all the turkey and dressing fixings out of here. I think it's better if it can sit in the fridge overnight."

Serves 8 to 10

Oven 350

Crust:
2 cups graham cracker crumbs
6 tablespoons butter, melted
3 tablespoons sugar

Filling:
2 (8 oz.) boxes cream cheese, softened
¾ cup sugar
3 eggs
1 cup canned pumpkin
¾ teaspoon cinnamon

Prepare crust by mixing ingredients together then firmly pressing mixture in greased spring form pan.

Mix the cream cheese and sugar together with mixer.

Add the 3 eggs – one at a time, mixing after each one.

Remove 1 cup of the filling plus 2 tablespoons and set both aside in separate bowls.

To the remaining mixture add the canned pumpkin and cinnamon and mix well.

Pour half of the pumpkin mixture over the crust.

Then pour 1 cup of the other plain mixture.

Top with the rest of the pumpkin mixture.

Use the remaining 2 tablespoons of plain mixture to achieve marbled effect. Do this by dipping a knife in the mixture and drawing parallel lines.
Maybe 8-10 lines.

Next drag a knife through the lines from left to right, repeat over the whole cheesecake alternating directions. (drag knife left to right, then right to left as you work your way down the cheesecake)

Bake for 35 minutes.

Completely cool, then refrigerate until you serve it.

Glazed Teacake
(CAN BE USED FOR PETIT FOURS)

Bea went around putting on the finishing touches. Her neat handwriting glided across the lavender place cards, and she carefully squeezed yellow flowers onto the corners of each homemade petit four cake.

Can be cut into 24 square pieces of cake

Oven 375

Cake:
2 cups flour
2 cups sugar
1 teaspoon baking powder
1 teaspoon salt
¼ teaspoon baking soda
1 cup butter, cubed
1 cup water
2 large eggs
½ cup sour cream
1 teaspoon almond extract

Frosting:
½ cup butter, cubed
¼ cup milk
4 ½ cups powdered sugar
½ teaspoon almond extract

Grease a 15x10x1 baking pan.

In a large bowl, whisk the flour, sugar, baking powder, salt and baking soda.

In a small saucepan, combine butter and water and bring just to a boil.

Stir into flour mixture.

In a small bowl whisk eggs, sour cream and almond extract until blended.

Add to flour mixture, mixing constantly.

Transfer to prepared pan. Bake 18-22 minutes until toothpick inserted in center comes out clean.

Cool on a wire rack for 20 minutes.

While cake is cooling make frosting by combining butter and milk in a large saucepan.

Bring just to a boil and remove from heat.

Gradually stir in powdered sugar and almond extract.

Spread over warm cake.

For petit fours cut into 24 squares and arrange on pretty tray. Use store-bought icing to decorate or use 1 cup powdered sugar, 1 tablespoon water and food color of your choice to make your own icing. (Add powdered sugar or water as needed to make it a thick, but smooth, consistency.) Decorate using pastry bag and decorating tip OR you can use a knife and/or toothpick to make polka dots or other designs.

Four Layer Dessert

I'm certain this is what Bea made for dessert when Winston and Molly Baker came to dinner. My mom has been making it for years and it never disappoints.

Serves 8 to 10

Layer 1:
1 cup flour
½ cup chopped pecans
1 tablespoon sugar
1 stick butter, melted

Mix ingredients together and press firmly into 9x13 glass baking dish.

Cook for 15 minutes at 350.

Let cool before adding other layers.

Layer 2:
8 oz. cream cheese, softened
1 cup powdered sugar
1 cup Cool Whip *(removed from 16 oz. container of Cool Whip)*

Mix ingredients together and spread over cooled crust.

Layer 3:
1 small package instant vanilla pudding
1 small package instant chocolate pudding
3 cups cold milk

Beat ingredients together with mixer then spread over cream cheese layer.

Layer 4:
Top with the rest of the container of Cool Whip.

Keep refrigerated.

Julie's Chocolate Chip Cookies

I served these at the book release party that my friends at The Lazy Dog Saloon in Ridgway, Colorado threw for me. I kept telling people at the party that my book is basically a love letter to their beautiful town.

Makes 36 cookies

Oven 375

2 ¼ cups flour
1 teaspoon baking soda
1 teaspoon salt
1 cup butter flavored shortening
¾ cup white sugar
¾ cup brown sugar
1 teaspoon vanilla
1 large egg
2 cups semi-sweet chocolate morsels
1 cup chopped pecans (optional)
1 tablespoon milk if needed

Mix all ingredients except morsels and nuts with mixer until just combined. Don't overmix because this puts too much air into the dough. Dough will be very stiff.

Add a tablespoon of milk if needed to make it easier to stir. You still want it pretty stiff, though.

Stir in chocolate morsels and chopped pecans if using.

Drop by rounded teaspoon onto ungreased baking sheets.

Bake for 10 minutes or until just starting to brown.

Let cool on baking sheet for 2 minutes then remove to wire rack to cool completely.

Note: I'm sort of known for my chocolate chip cookies. After years of making the Tollhouse recipe, I finally admitted that I thought they could be improved upon. There was something too cakey about them. So, I took it upon myself to make some improvements.

ABOUT THE AUTHOR

JULIE ADKISON has wanted to write a novel for as long as she can remember. She has written poems and short stories and has taken many creative writing classes over the years. She did a stint on "Music Row" as a songwriter (Jason Aldean, Terri Clark, Sixwire, Point of Grace, film & TV), and she wrote a cookbook with some friends (*Cooking with Grace* with Point of Grace). But none of these things scratched her itch to write a novel.

Her love of writing intersects with her love of the southwest region of Colorado in this debut novel. It is referred to as the "Switzerland of America." There is nowhere as inspiring as this place where she has been traveling since childhood.

Julie's other interests include musical theatre (proud theatre mom), cooking, snow skiing and travel. She lives in La Vergne, Tennessee, just outside her hometown of Nashville. Her most important roles are wife to Mark, mom to Sydney and dog mom to Maisy and Sadie.

CimarronFalls.com • Julietheauthor.com